John Foster and Korky Paul
DRAGON POEMS

Oxford University Press

Oxford   New York   Toronto

For Tessa : K.P.

Oxford University Press, Walton Street, Oxford OX2 6DP
Oxford New York Toronto
Delhi Bombay Calcutta Madras Karachi
Petaling Jaya Singapore Hong Kong Tokyo
Nairobi Dar es Salaam Cape Town
Melbourne Auckland

and associated companies in
Berlin Ibadan

Oxford is a trade mark of Oxford University Press

This selection and arrangement © John Foster 1991

Illustrations © Korky Paul 1991

First published 1991

ISBN 019 276096 3

A CIP catalogue reference for this book is available from the British
Library

Set by FWT Studios, England

Printed in Hong Kong

Acknowledgements

The editor and publisher are grateful for permission to include the
following copyright material in this anthology.

Moira Andrew, 'Portrait of a Dragon', © by Moira Andrew.
Reprinted by permission of the author.

Tony Bradman, 'The Pet', © 1991 by Tony Bradman. Reprinted by
permission of the author.

Max Fatchen, 'Anyone Wanting a Fiery Dragon' from *A Paddock of
Poems* (Omnibus/Puffin, Adelaide 1987) © Max Fatchen 1987.
Reprinted by permission of John Johnson Ltd.

Eric Finney, 'Dragon Band' and 'The Ice Dragons', © 1991 by Eric
Finney. Reprinted by permission of the author.

John Foster, 'The School for Young Dragons', © 1991 by John
Foster.

David Harmer, 'Never Trust Dragons' © 1991 by David Harmer.
Reprinted by permission of the author.

Julie Holder, 'How Dragons Hide', 'The Lonely Dragon', 'Is There a
Dragon in the House?', © 1991 by Julie Holder.

X. J. Kennedy, 'My Dragon' from *The Phantom Ice-Cream Man*
(1979), © 1975, 1977, 1978, 1979 by X. J. Kennedy. Reprinted by
permission of Curtis Brown Ltd.

Ian Larmont, 'The Last Dragon', © 1991 by Ian Larmont. Reprinted
by permission of the author.

Daphne Lister 'The Dragon' from *Gingerbread Pigs & Other Rhymes*
(Transworld 1980). © by Daphne Lister. Reprinted by permission of
the author.

Lilian Moore, 'Lost and Found' from *See My Lovely Poison Ivy*, ©
1975 by Lilian Moore. Reprinted by permission of Marian Reiner for
the author.

Judith Nicholls, 'Dragonbirth', © 1991 by Judith Nicholls. Reprinted
by permission of the author.

Jack Prelutsky, 'Happy Birthday, Dear Dragon' from *The New Kid
On The Block,* © 1984 by Jack Prelutsky. Reprinted by permission of
William Heinemann Ltd., and Greenwillow Books, William Morrow
& Co. Inc.

Irene Rawnsley, 'Dragon's Breath' from *Dog's Dinner*, by Irene
Rawnsley. Reprinted by permission of Methuen Childrens Books.

William Jay Smith, 'The Toaster' from *Laughing Time,* © 1955,
1957, 1980, 1990 by William Jay Smith. Reprinted by permission of
Farrar Straus & Giroux Inc.

Charles Thomson, 'A Dragon in the Classroom', © 1991 Charles
Thomson. Reprinted by permission of the author.

Clive Webster, 'No Contest', 'Drawback', © 1991 by Clive Webster,
Reprinted by permission of the author.

Colin West, 'Jocelyn, My Dragon' from *The Best of West* (Hutchinson
1990) ©1990 by Colin West. Reprinted by permission of the author.

Raymond Wilson, 'The Grateful Dragon' © 1991 by Raymond
Wilson. Reprinted by permission of the author.

CONTENTS

4

Happy Birthday, Dear Dragon

There were rumbles of strange jubilation
in a dark, subterranean lair,
for the dragon was having a birthday,
and his colleagues were gathering there.
'**HOORAH!**' groaned the trolls and the ogres
as they pelted each other with stones.
'HOORAH!' shrieked a sphinx and a griffin,
and the skeletons rattled their bones.

'HOORAH!' screamed the queen of the demons.
'HOORAH!' boomed a giant. 'REJOICE!'
'**Hoorah!**' piped a tiny hobgoblin
in an almost inaudible voice.
'HOORAH!' cackled rapturous witches.
'*Hoorahhhhhhh!*' hissed a basilisk too.
Then they howled in cacophonous chorus,
'HAPPY BIRTHDAY,
DEAR DRAGON,
TO YOU!'

They whistled, they squawked, they applauded,
as they gleefully brought forth the cake.
'**OH, THANK YOU!**'
he thundered with pleasure
in a bass that made every ear ache.
Then puffing his chest to the fullest,
and taking deliberate aim,
the dragon huffed once at the candles –

and
the candles
all burst
into
flame!

Jack Prelutsky

6

Portrait of a Dragon

If I were an artist
I'd paint the portrait
of a dragon.

To do a proper job
I'd borrow colours
from the world.

For his back I'd
need a mountain range,
all misty-blue.

For spikes I'd use
dark fir trees pointing
to the sky.

For overlapping scales
I'd squeeze dye from
bright anemones.

I'd gild his claws
like shining swords
with starlight.

His tail would be
a river, silver
in the sun.

For his head, the
secret green of forests
and deep seas.

And his eyes would
glow like embers in
a tinker's fire.

But I'd keep the best
till last. For his
hot breath

I'd use all reds and
yellows – crocus, saffron,
peony, poppy,

geranium, cyclamen, rose –
and fierce orange flames
from a marigold.

Moira Andrew

The Pet

My mum gave me some money
   To buy myself a treat;
She said I could buy anything
   (So long as it wasn't sweets).

So off I went to spend it.
   I wandered round the shops,
I couldn't find a thing to buy . . .
   Then something made me stop.

There in a pet shop window
   I saw a flash of fire;
I saw some scales and burning eyes
   And I knew my heart's desire.

I gave the man my money.
   He handed me a lead.
Then I walked out of the pet shop
   With the only pet I need.

A pet with wings and gleaming fangs,
   With skin that's shiny green;
With claws, and a tail that's longer
   Than any tail you've seen.

A pet whose breath is orange flame,
   Whose ears both hiss with steam,
Who'll fly me to the land of clouds
   And to the land of dreams.

But first I'd better go home.
   I hope that it's OK . . .
I hope my mum will like my pet.
   I wonder what she'll say?

Tony Bradman

No Contest

The little boy was in distress –
'Dad,' he yelled. 'Quick, help!
A fiery dragon's just got Mum,
She's fighting it herself.'

'Don't worry, son,' his dad replied,
Ignoring his son's pleading.
'The dragon's in with half a chance'–
And carried on his reading.

Clive Webster

My Dragon

I have a purple dragon
With a long brass tail that clangs,
And anyone not nice to me
Soon feels his fiery fangs,

So if you tell me I'm a dope
Or call my muscles jelly,
You just might dwell a billion years
Inside his boiling belly.

X. J. Kennedy

A Dragon in the Classroom

There's a dragon in the classroom:
its body is a box,
its head's a plastic waste-bin,
its eyes are broken clocks,

its legs are cardboard tubes,
its claws are toilet rolls,
its tongue's my dad's old tie
(that's why it's full of holes).

'Oh, what a lovely dragon,'
our teacher smiled and said.
'You *are* a pretty dragon,'
she laughed and stroked its head.

'Oh no, I'm not,' he snorted,
SNAP! SNAP! he moved his jaw
and chased our screaming teacher
along the corridor.

Charles Thomson

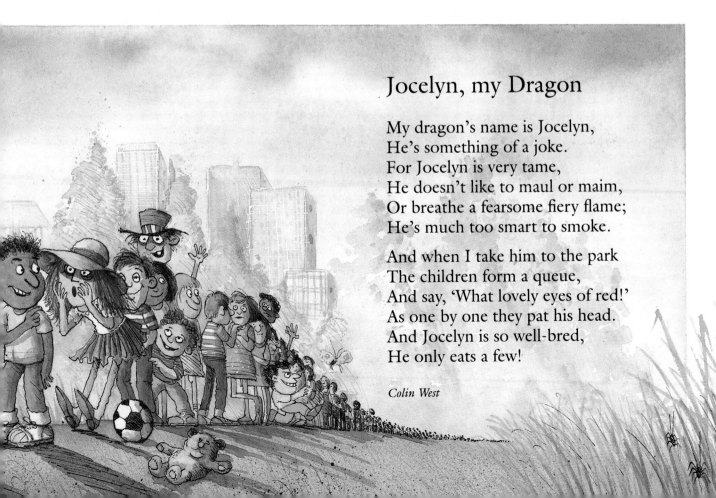

Jocelyn, my Dragon

My dragon's name is Jocelyn,
He's something of a joke.
For Jocelyn is very tame,
He doesn't like to maul or maim,
Or breathe a fearsome fiery flame;
He's much too smart to smoke.

And when I take him to the park
The children form a queue,
And say, 'What lovely eyes of red!'
As one by one they pat his head.
And Jocelyn is so well-bred,
He only eats a few!

Colin West

Dragonbirth

*In the midnight mists
of long ago
on a far-off mountainside
there stood
a wild oak wood . . .*

In the wild, wet wood
there grew an oak;
beneath the oak
there slept a cave
and in that cave
the mosses crept.
Beneath the moss
there lay a stone,
beneath the stone
there lay an egg,
and in that egg
there was a crack.
From that crack
there breathed a flame;
from that flame
there burst a fire,
and from that fire

dragon came.

Judith Nicholls

Dragon's Breath

One winter
when the world was still
a dragon came into the cold;
he rattled all the icicles
and shook his scales of gold.

He spread his body on the earth
to make the flowers grow;
he snorted
with his fiery breath
and melted all the snow.

He snorted
with his fiery breath
to set the river free;
he coiled his golden tail
around a budding hazel tree.

He coiled his golden tail
until catkins began to shake,
then spread his wings
and flew
to warm another world awake.

Irene Rawnsley

How Dragons Hide

Dragon babies
Are fat and pudgy
They slide down the helter-skelter
Of Mother Dragon's back
They swing on her tail
They pull faces at themselves
In the mirror of her scales.

Dragon babies
Bibble and babble
They blow smoke bubbles
They dribble small flames
They suck sun hot pebbles
And crunch them in sharp little teeth.

Dragon babies
Play with jingly jewels
They leave them where they fall
To become buried treasure
They throw them in the river
To see the splashes.

Dragon babies
Clap their small wings
Pretending they are old enough to fly
They roll in the river mud
To make small clouds of steam.
Their Mother lies like a low green hill
And watches over them.

If they hear the sounds of people
They hide in the long green grass
Still as stones they lie
Their Mother hides her head
And becomes a low green hill.

They hold their fiery breath
And the people pass
Seeing only stones in the grass
And a low green hill.

Julie Holder

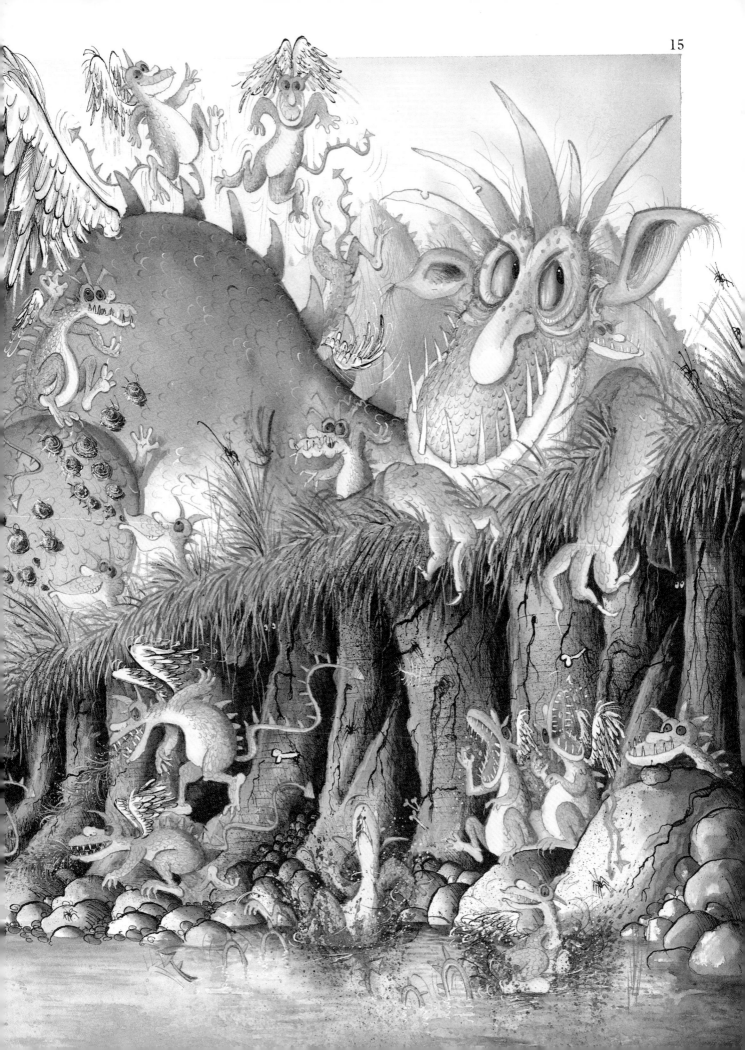

16

The School for Young Dragons

At the school for young dragons
The main lessons are
Flying and feasting and fighting.

In flying they learn
How to take off and land
How to dive and to swoop
How to loop the loop
And how to leave trails of sky-writing.

In feasting they learn
About how to behave
When invited to dine
In an old dragon's cave.
They learn that it's rude
To gobble your food,
That you should not belch fire
That you must always sit up straight
And never, ever, scorch your plate.

In fighting they learn
How to scare off their foes
With jets of flame
That will singe their toes,
How to puff a smoke screen
So they cannot be seen.
How a knight with a lance
Hasn't much of a chance
Against dragons who know
How a whack of the tail
Can shatter chain-mail.

At the school for young dragons
The main lessons are
Flying and feasting and fighting,
Which is why you will hear
A young dragon say
'Our lessons are really exciting!
It's better than reading and writing!'

John Foster

SCHOOL
FOR YOUNG
DRAGONS
NO KNIGHTS

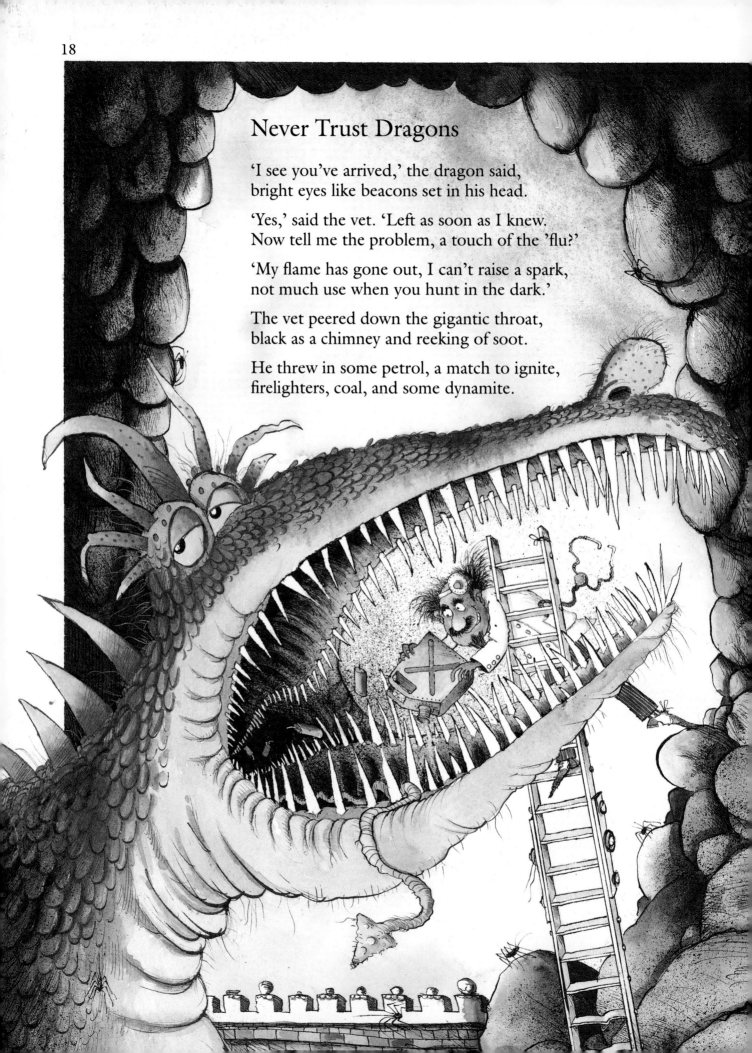

Never Trust Dragons

'I see you've arrived,' the dragon said,
bright eyes like beacons set in his head.

'Yes,' said the vet. 'Left as soon as I knew.
Now tell me the problem, a touch of the 'flu?'

'My flame has gone out, I can't raise a spark,
not much use when you hunt in the dark.'

The vet peered down the gigantic throat,
black as a chimney and reeking of soot.

He threw in some petrol, a match to ignite,
firelighters, coal, and some dynamite.

The dragon covered a burp with his paw,
a flicker of flame flashed down his jaw.

He licked his lips with a golden tongue:
'Take your fee, vet, you'd better run.

I can feel my fires boil, they are returning.
In a couple of minutes you could be burning.'

Clutching a diamond the size of a star,
the vet scampered away to his car.

As he drove off the dragon's bright fires
gushed out of the cave and scorched his tyres.

The vet snapped his fingers, laughed at the brute
because he was wearing his flame-proof suit.

David Harmer

Lost and Found

LOST:
A Wizard's loving pet.
Rather longish.
Somewhat scaly.
May be hungry or
upset.
Please feed daily.

P. S. Reward.

THIS BEAST
FOR
SALE

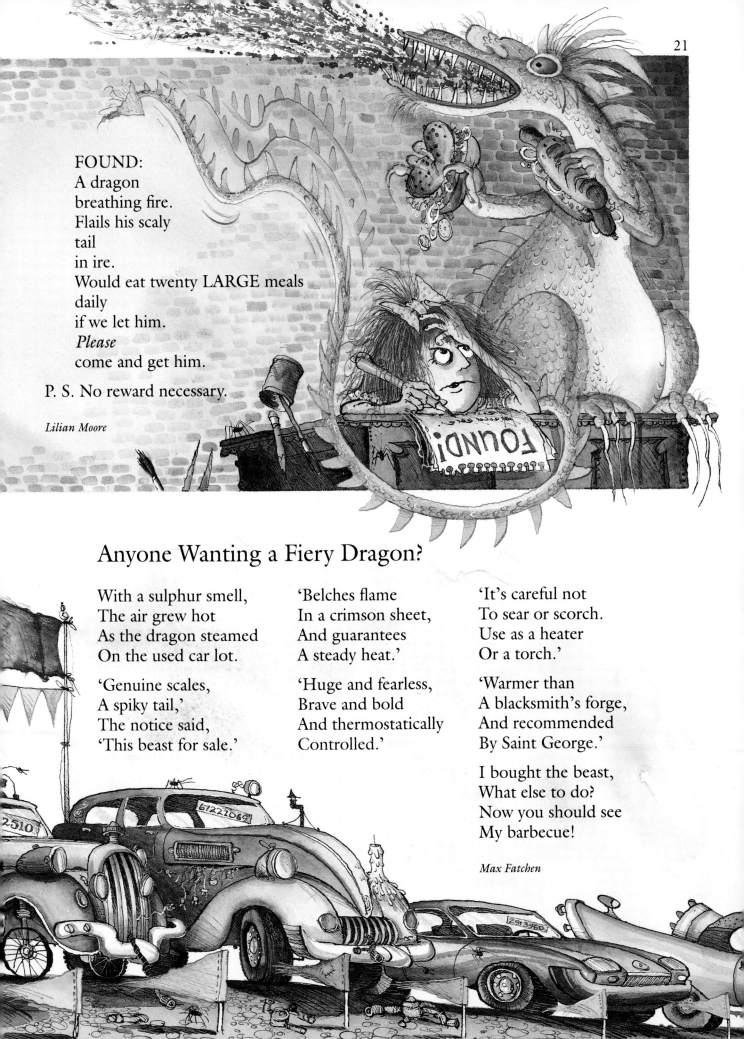

FOUND:
A dragon
breathing fire.
Flails his scaly
tail
in ire.
Would eat twenty LARGE meals
daily
if we let him.
Please
come and get him.

P. S. No reward necessary.

Lilian Moore

Anyone Wanting a Fiery Dragon?

With a sulphur smell,
The air grew hot
As the dragon steamed
On the used car lot.

'Genuine scales,
A spiky tail,'
The notice said,
'This beast for sale.'

'Belches flame
In a crimson sheet,
And guarantees
A steady heat.'

'Huge and fearless,
Brave and bold
And thermostatically
Controlled.'

'It's careful not
To sear or scorch.
Use as a heater
Or a torch.'

'Warmer than
A blacksmith's forge,
And recommended
By Saint George.'

I bought the beast,
What else to do?
Now you should see
My barbecue!

Max Fatchen

The Toaster

A silver-scaled Dragon with jaws flaming red
Sits at my elbow and toasts my bread.
I hand him fat slices, and then, one by one,
He hands them back when he sees they are done.

William Jay Smith

Drawback

The dragon raged with flame and fire,
He blew it down his nose –
But the poor old soul was quite cross-eyed
And burnt off all his toes.

Clive Webster

Dragon Band

It's the best in the land,
The Dragon Band:
There's **Gnorda**
On recorder,
Gondar
On guitar,
Dronga
On the bonger
And the big Oompah;
Dorgan
Plays the organ,
And **Ardong**
Sings a song
(It does drag on a bit,
It's much too long!)
G. Darno plays piano,
Giving it a bash,
And **Randgo**
Twangs a banjo
With great panache.
When they get it
All together
It's grand, **O grand!**
It's the latest,
It's the greatest,
It's the Dragon Band!

Eric Finney

Is there a Dragon in the House?

I visited a castle
One summer afternoon.
I didn't want to join the crowd,
So I wandered off alone
Over the creaking drawbridge
Past the tower keep,
And in a courtyard
On the cobbles
I came upon a Dragon –
Yes, a Dragon –
Fast asleep.

I could see that it was sleeping
And not a ghost or dead,
For I saw it gently breathing
And it flicked its heavy ears
Against the flies that buzzed its head.

I tiptoed up to touch it
For curiosity
And proof.
And its scales were rough as the bark of a tree
And thick as tiles on a roof.

Then the crowd came round the corner
And the crowd's guide said,
'And it's here in this very courtyard
That a Knight fought a terrible Dragon
And the Dragon dropped down dead.'

The Dragon opened yellow eyes,
It yawned and stretched and blinked,
And over the heads of the guide and crowd
It looked
At me
And winked.

'Oh, no. Not dead,'
The Dragon said,
'That isn't Dragon lore.'
But no one else there heard it speak,
No one else there saw.

'As sure as grass is green,'
The Dragon said,
'As sure as daisies grow,
Dragons do not die,
They simply come and go.
They come and go as surely
As heroes in tin will dent.'
Then it grinned and waved its tail
And then the Dragon
Went.

The crowd moved on behind the guide
Through a narrow castle door.
They clattered, scuffed and tripped
The cobbled courtyard floor,
But none of those feet
Rubbed out the print,
The print of the Dragon's paw.

The print of its paw
On the cobbles
Left behind to show
That Dragons do not die
They simply come and go.

This story is for Dragons,
For I've never thought it right
That Dragons should be invented
To make a hero of a Knight.

Julie Holder

The Grateful Dragon

A dragon crawled to the castle door
  and everyone inside
looked down on it from the castle walls,
  curious but terrified.

It was half the size of a football pitch,
  bright green, with spots of red,
but it hadn't the strength to lash its tail
  and lay there, as if dead.

The Winter had turned the woods to iron,
  the snow was deep as a house;
there wasn't a blade of grass to be seen
  nor a skinny harvest mouse.

'It's starving!' the King cried. 'Now's our chance!'
  looking down from the castle wall –
'Bring lances and crossbows and arrows
  and let's kill it, once for all.'

The dragon was too weak to move
  more than an eyelid, and yet
the Princess saw a tear form there and it
  moved her heart with regret.

'Please spare the dragon!' the Princess begged.
  'Put out some bundles of hay.
Once it's grown strong from eating it will
  harmlessly go away.'

The King looked hard in his daughter's face
  and saw how much she cared,
then nodded that they should do as she asked,
  and so the dragon was spared.

Next Autumn brought enemy soldiers.
  The King and his subjects shut
themselves in the castle, and there they starved
  while the harvest stayed uncut.

The Princess wept on the castle wall
  when suddenly there came
in a whirlwind of thunder and fury
  the dragon, spouting flame.

The enemy soldiers ran off in fright
  and never again were seen;
and the people came out of the castle
  and gathered the harvest in.

Raymond Wilson

The Lonely Dragon

He lives in the mouth of a mountain
Behind the teeth of mist,
He sighs at the thought
Of the Knights he's not fought
And the maidens he never has kissed.

He sprawls in a nest of treasure,
Plays fivestones with rubies and pearls.
On the back of his paw he wipes his nose,
And idly on his rattling toes
The crown of a King he twirls.

He belches and scratches his belly,
He is bored with before and behind him.
He spits sparks to the dark and sings rude songs,
His roars shake the mountain tops like blancmange,
But only the spiders mind him.

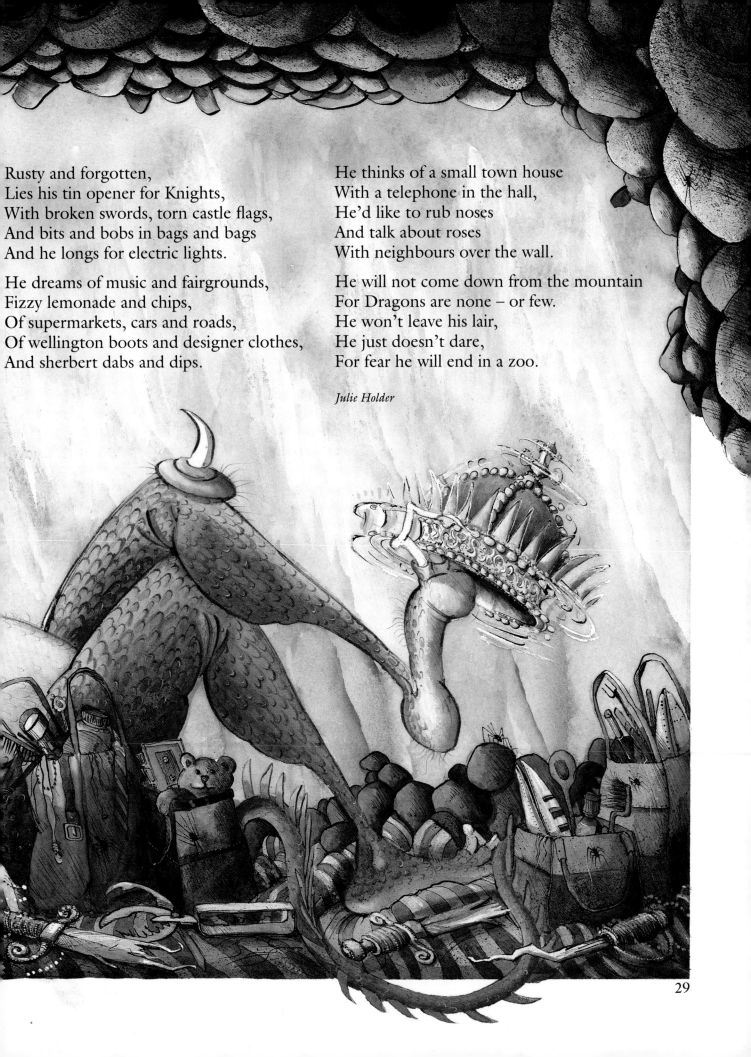

Rusty and forgotten,
Lies his tin opener for Knights,
With broken swords, torn castle flags,
And bits and bobs in bags and bags
And he longs for electric lights.

He dreams of music and fairgrounds,
Fizzy lemonade and chips,
Of supermarkets, cars and roads,
Of wellington boots and designer clothes,
And sherbert dabs and dips.

He thinks of a small town house
With a telephone in the hall,
He'd like to rub noses
And talk about roses
With neighbours over the wall.

He will not come down from the mountain
For Dragons are none – or few.
He won't leave his lair,
He just doesn't dare,
For fear he will end in a zoo.

Julie Holder

29

The Dragon

I saw a cloud like a dragon,
Lying in wait in the sky,
With a purple head and a purple tail
And a little blue patch for an eye.

From his snout came flames of fire,
And he began to run,
Chasing the daylight away to the west
And fighting the setting sun!

Daphne Lister

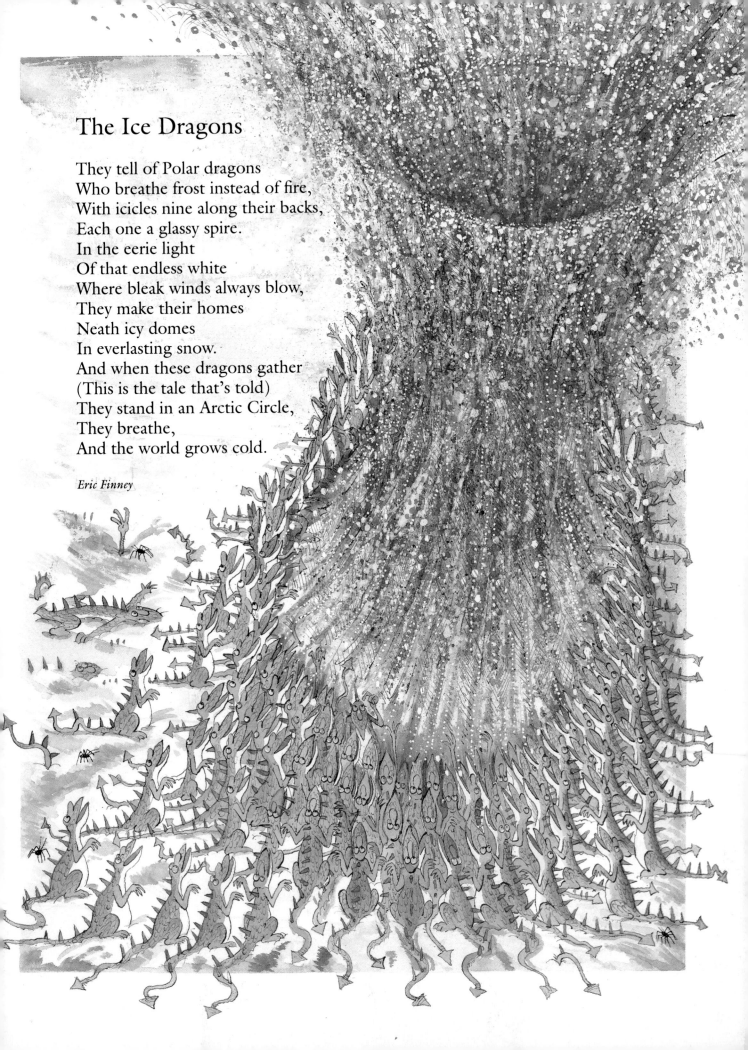

The Ice Dragons

They tell of Polar dragons
Who breathe frost instead of fire,
With icicles nine along their backs,
Each one a glassy spire.
In the eerie light
Of that endless white
Where bleak winds always blow,
They make their homes
Neath icy domes
In everlasting snow.
And when these dragons gather
(This is the tale that's told)
They stand in an Arctic Circle,
They breathe,
And the world grows cold.

Eric Finney

The Last Dragon

Beneath a high mountain,
Inside a dark cave,
A crusty old dragon,
As cold as the grave.

As cold as the high,
Vaulted stone overhead.
As cold as the gold
That is spilled as his bed.

The last of the dragons.
There will be no more.
And slow beats his heart
On his glittering store.

The beating gets slower
As life drifts away.
A hundred more lifetimes
Just pass as a day.

At last a low moan
Where there once was a roar.
The last of the dragons
Is breathing no more.

Ian Larmont